Bob Saget's
Tales from the Crib

with Tony Hendra

A Perigee Book

Perigee Books
are published by
The Putnam Publishing Group
200 Madison Avenue
New York, NY 10016

Library of Congress Cataloging-in-Publication Data

Saget, Bob.
(Tales from the crib)
Bob Saget's Tales from the crib/Bob Saget with Tony Hendra.
p. cm.
ISBN 0-399-51676-X
1. Children — Caricatures and cartoons. 2. American wit and humor,
Pictorial. I. Hendra, Tony. II. Title. III. Title: Tales from the crib.
NC1429.S315A4   1991   90-24951 CIP
741.5' 973 — dc20

Printed in the United States of America
1 2 3 4 5 6 7 8 9 10

This book is printed on acid-free paper.
∞

Credits and Acknowledgments:

EDITED BY: TONY HENDRA
WRITTEN BY: BOB SAGET AND TONY HENDRA
ART DIRECTION AND COVER DESIGN BY: JAN ULRIK LETH

Assistant to the Editor: Catherine Curran
Cover Photography: Steve Prezant (New York) Ken Stapleton (L.A.)
Cover Retouching: Bob Rakita

Special thanks to Judy Linden for her patience and support.
Thanks also to: Sharon Stahl, Bob Tabian, Ray Reo,
Peter Bonventre, David Fischer, Roger Neal,
Gina Godoy, Graydon and Spike Carter,
and the inventor of the fax machine.

Foreword

Hi there. This is a picture book about a subject which my friend Tony and I hold dear to our hearts—little kids. Every time I communicate with a baby who can't respond to me verbally, I try to make them laugh with weird sounds and rude noises. But you can't help but wonder...If they could talk, would their jokes be funny? Would they have good timing?

It really bugs me that people underestimate the intelligence of babies and condescend to them. The only difference between a baby and myself is five feet and a pound and a half of hair. Also they just aren't programmed with all their data yet. That's what this book is all about...programming little ones with enough cultural data to evoke laughter.

The concept of this book is obviously a familiar one. Hieroglyphics have actually been found, dating from prehistoric cultures which depict "cave babies" with funny captions underneath. Famous artists from the Renaissance painted elaborate baby portraits, with funny captions under them, but the "powers that be" forced them to remove the captions because it was felt they "cheapened the fine art." Okay, I made up all that, but the point is, for as far back as there have been babies, people have tried to put words in their mouths.

To get these photos we asked moms and dads (and other assorted relatives) across America for their funniest baby photos. As we looked at over thirty-thousand photos, one thing stood out — every shot was taken with lots of love, a sense of humor, and a disposable camera — no, I'm kidding, they were good cameras. But what are those disposable cameras all about? Can you shave with them after you shoot a roll?..perhaps not. Anyway, thank you parents...thank you children, too...and you know what? Since I've gotten overly sappy, I'd like to thank my mom and dad for only taking four lousy baby pictures of me because I was their third child. I'm sorry, that's not true, there's a giant four-foot picture of me wearing a goofy baseball suit and sporting a buzz-cut hanging in their living room. If you want to see it, they charge admission...

But enough about my childhood, it's time now to peek into the minds of some of the cutest kids ever assembled in one paperback...Oh, and thanks for reading the foreword. I usually skip this stuff.

This Book is Dedicated to All Our Children

TWIN ☾CHEEKS

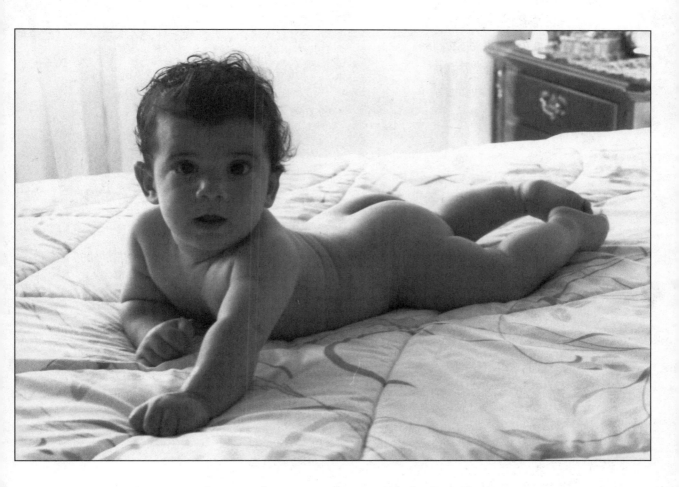

Hi! Welcome to the seamy, steamy world of... Twin Cheeks!
Beneath the surface of our apparently normal little
community, power and passion bubble like lava under Krakatoa.
I'm **BENJAMIN FONTANEL,**
merciless millionaire and heartless heel.
Right now I'm romancing the socks off...

...star-crossed, cat-food heiress **JOSIE HAUTE-BASSINET,** currently recovering in the local sanitarium from a ten-day, round- the-world rampage after she was abandoned at the altar rails by...

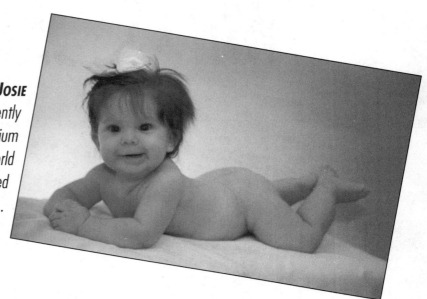

...her high-school sweetheart, big-hearted basketball jock and ex-sheriff of Twin Cheeks, **JOCK FONTANEL.** Slamdunked by a friend at his bachelor party, **JOCK** now has amnesia and thinks he's a taxidermist named **MR. FIST** whose only mission in life is to marry...

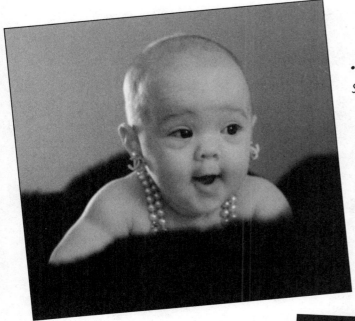

...ARMANDINE "HAPPY" THRUSH III, the spider at the center of Twin Cheeks' social web. **HAPPY** sashays around town in her Blackglama and nothing else. She's the only person who knows **JOSIE'S** dark secret: thanks to a cradle swap **JOSIE** isn't heir to the **HAUTE-BASSINET** cat-food fortune. The heir in fact is a woman **HAPPY** is blackmailing with a recipe-box full of compromising photos...

...breath-taking, tragic, international cosmetics model, **OPHELIA NAILS,** a multiple personality whose various identities include **JOE MONTANA** and a **ROLLS-ROYCE HOOD ORNAMENT. OPHELIA** is currently in jail for impersonating...

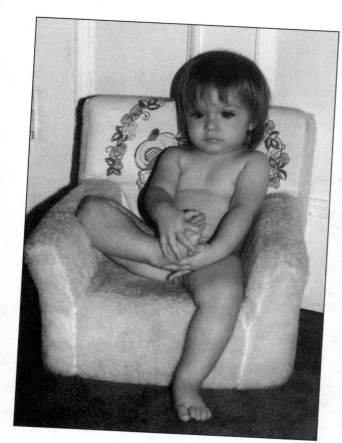

...my saintly sister, **FLAME FONTANEL**. **FLAME** runs the local soup-kitchen, runaway shelter and anti-pollution fund. Not that I give a damn about **MISS GOODY TWO-SHOES**...in fact I find it mildly amusing that **FLAME** locked herself in her room three weeks ago, pining for the love of...

...hard-hat hunk **HOMER NICKERSOFF**, whose family belongs to a fanatical sect that has kidnapped him to a remote mountain cabin, to "escape the Flame of Hell." **HOMER'S** also lost his job at the copper-mine due to the influence of **FLAME'S** other admirer...

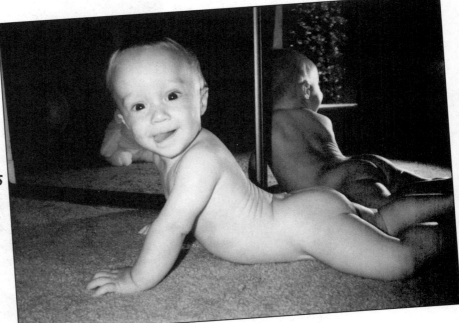

...insanely jealous **PALEY R. MURROW,** local media mogul and owner of the sensational tabloid INSIDE TWIN CHEEKS. **PALEY** is a ruthless entrepreneur who has vowed to own the town "from the outskirts to the inseam" but he is under investigation by...

...sultry District Attorney and interior decorator, **KATYA FELLON**, whose investigation stalled when she found herself hopelessly falling for the flamboyant **PALEY**, perhaps because she can't erase the memory of...

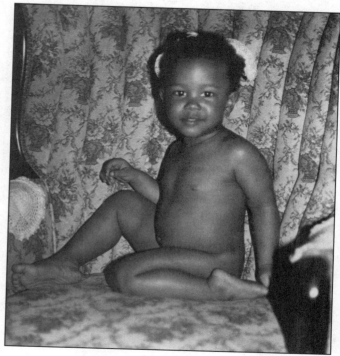

...her former fiance, **PALEY'S** twin brother **DALEY,** a passionate environmentalist, who suffers from amnesia thanks to falling off a log. He roams the local mountains as **DERMOT THE HERMIT**, a woodlands recluse who talks to the trees and removes thorns from the paws of animals like the Golden Retriever of...

...country singer **RUSTY NOBBS**, who saw **DALEY** running away after de-thorning her dog, fell in love with him and wrote a No.1 country single about the entire incident. Now she cannot find the nature boy she loves, who happens to be the catalyst of her fame. She has enlisted the powers of...

...old Hopi soothsayer, **DONA JUANA NO,** to cast a spell on **DALEY** by making him drink a love potion (if she can find him). But **DONA JUANA** has gotten the love potion mixed up with a deadly, untraceable poison she concocted for...

...local mobster **NOODLES CHIANTI** (seen here in a police "wanted" photo). **NOODLES** is planning a hit on **DONA JUANA'S** secret lover...

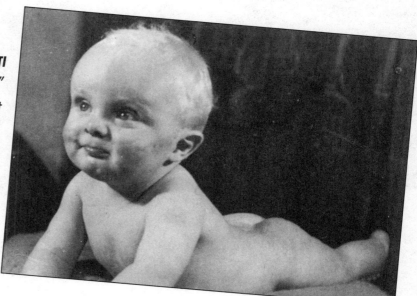

...philanthropist and international silk merchant **ADAM KOLLICK**. To carry out the hit, **NOODLES** hired the services of...

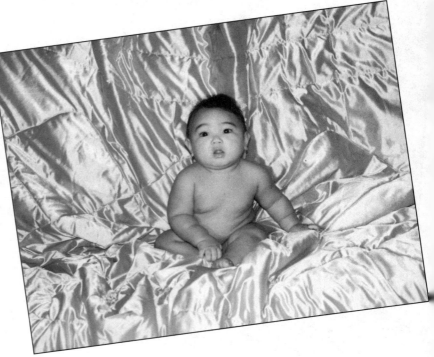

...the notorious **BUNN BROTHERS,** all of whom got the hit in the head during their last job, have amnesia and think they're in the chorus line of **THE BOB FOSSE STORY...**

...tune in tomorrow for love, passion, beginnings, and of course ends, on the Baby Soap of our times...
TWIN CHEEKS!

THE
MEN'S
CLUB

MR. ROMNEY
Chairman
Enthusiastic; gregarious; liberal spender; longest tab
in Club bar; bold use of Club funds. "I'm telling you--
junk bonds have bottomed out!"

MR. VAN NUS

Oldest member
Given to lengthy stories of
"the good old days."

MR. BURKE
Food & Beverage Committee
Club cut-up; large stock of
risque limericks.

MR. DILLON

Entertainment Committee
Reserved; bachelor; succeeded in booking
Carol Channing for upcoming smoker.

MR. BURTON

Vice Chairman
Club playboy; a Rolodex full of
debutantes; "Hey cupcake,
wanna tango?"

MR. HENRY

Poker Committee

Never cracks a smile; insists on a new deck
every game; "No smoking, no drinking...
this is serious business."

MR. POPKO

Club Librarian
Very definite tastes; "Nothing racy
in <u>this</u> library!"

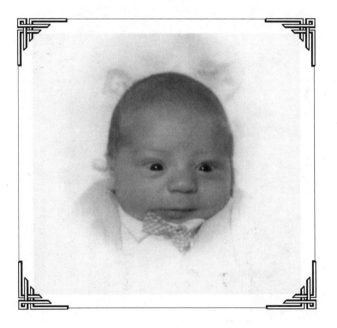

MR. SACKETT
Newest Member (and smallest)
Generous, outgoing, athletic.
World class skier.

MR. BADGER

Treasurer
Pressing obligations at home;
regrets that he cannot attend
recent meetings.

MR. MARTIN
Security Committee
Not much known about him;
very reliable.

MR. DUVA
Expelled for unseemly and
ungentlemanly behavior on
club picnic.

MR. THILMAN

Public Relations

A gladhander; free with gifts
and gratuities to city officials.

SOME OF YOUR BODIES - PREFERABLY THE ONES WITH TWO BUMPS IN THE FRONT - HAVE BEEN SELECTED AS THE MEANS BY WHICH WE INTEND TO ENTER YOUR DIMENSION. WE WILL TAKE OVER EACH OF THESE BODIES FOR A PERIOD OF APPROXIMATELY NINE MONTHS, BY WHICH TIME THE TWO BUMPS WILL HAVE REACHED AN UNEARTHLY SIZE...

STAGE TWO: WE WILL ENTER YOUR HOMES WHERE YOU WILL FEED US, CLOTHE US AND TEND TO OUR EVERY NEED 24 HOURS A DAY. WE WILL APPEAR TO BE HARMLESS AND NON-THREATENING. HOWEVER, DURING THIS TIME WE WILL UTTERLY DISRUPT YOUR LIFESTYLES, SOCIAL ACTIVITIES, LONG-TERM GOALS, CAREER COMMITMENTS, CHERISHED BELIEFS, SLEEPING PATTERNS AND DIGESTIVE SYSTEMS...

WHEN I GROW UP I WANT TO BE...

Coach John Madden

WHEN I GROW UP I WANT TO BE...

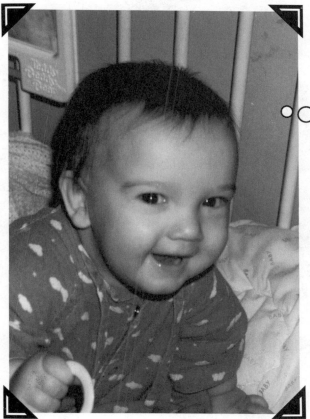

WHEN I GROW UP I WANT TO BE...

Mel Torme

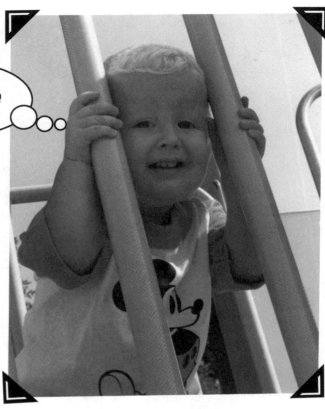

Jane Curtin

Paul Sorvino

Phil Collins

When I grow up I want to be...

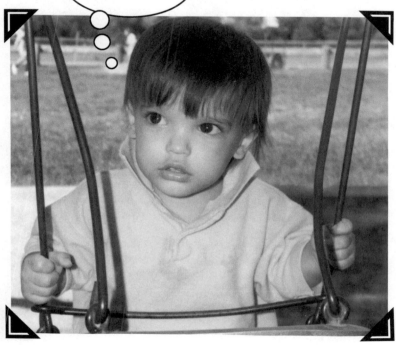

Danny Kaye

Vic Damone

WHEN I GROW UP I WANT TO BE...

62

Buddy Hackett

A Thanksgiving Day Special:

MY POINTER SAYS "WALK THIS WAY"

YOU FIND SUCH NEAT STUFF IN THE NEIGHBOR'S GARBAGE.

The

Ladies' Club

MS. LAUREN

Chairperson, President, CEO

The more meetings the merrier.
Stickler for Robert's Rules of Order.
Iron fist in velvet glove.

"A club cannot be a democracy without a strong leader."

Ms. Johnson

Treasurer

Free spirit; spends with no guilt.
Three new outfits a day. Successfully squashed misuse-of-club-funds investigation.
First cousin of Chairperson Lauren.

"Charge it! Charge it! CHARGE IT!"

MS. BULLOCK

Director, Bible Study Program

Cautious to a fault; appreciates any kind of constructive input.

"Exactly which bible should we be studying?"

Ms. Zaba

Editor, Club Newsletter

Knows how to work a room; queen of innuendo.

"Darlings, have you heard? Someone at the tippy-top of this club may be having **liposuction**…*"*

MS. ALLEN

Cotillion Committee

Much too pretty for her own good;
crazy about fans (of all kinds).

*"I'm not complaining, but I have so many admirers,
I have to beat them off with a polo mallet."*

MS. MCMILLAN

Club Historian

Files, files, files;
an expert on the past...
She lives it, breathes it, wears it.

"The only value of the present is that it becomes the past."

Ms. Burnham

Chairman, Pie Committee

A deep-dish, golden-crust kind of girl.

"Not a meeting goes by, without a slice of my pie."

MS. RYNO

Director, Health and Fitness

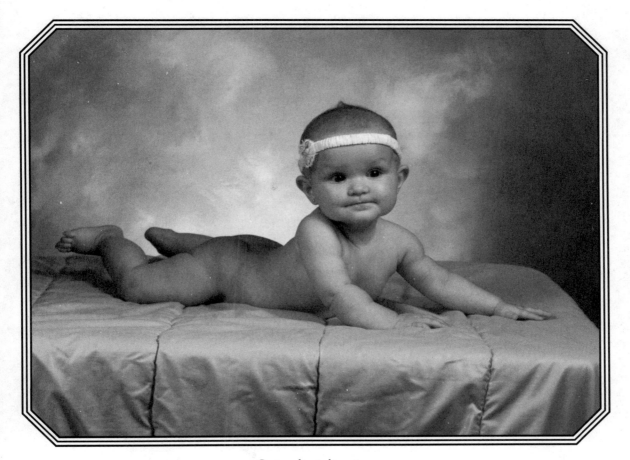

Strict disciplinarian.
Believes women can equal or exceed
men's upper-body strength. Casual dresser.

"Take care of your upper body, and your mind will take care of itself."

MS. COOEY

Chairman, Easter Bonnet Committee

Headgear is her life.

"All the well-dressed woman really needs is a hat."

MS. GORDON

Chairman, Entertainment Committee

Ex-model, ex-aerobics instructor,
ex-airline pilot, former executive.
Everybody's buddy, party animal, loosey-goosey.
Always the last to leave.

"Why should boys have all the fun?"

MS. LANOUX

Recording Secretary

Club mascot. Everybody's darling.
Loves her work.
Occasional lapses in accuracy.

"Minits of Klub meating June 32nd."

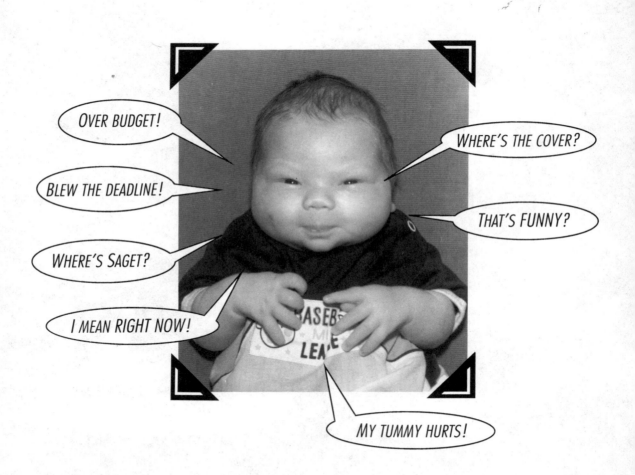

Index

Allen Chelsea, page 82
Anthony, Evan 40
Armagost, Alex 25
Babis, Grant 69
Bachman, Derek Ronald 45
Bachman, Kyle August 45
Badger, Chase E. 36
Bakhit, Charlie 15
Balmer, Ursula 59
Bayles, Kyle 75
photographer Bonita Pietila
Berk, Emily Lauren 78
Berzner, Bianca 91
photographer Jeanne Berzner
Bifulco, Allessandra 41
photographer Marie Bifulco
Borr, Shela 17
Bright, Justin 9
Bright, Zachery 9
Bristow, Karisha Catherine 13
Brundige, Joseph 42
Buczek, Mikhail 61
Bullock, Natalie Marie 80
Burke, Connor 30
photographer Marianne Burke
Burnham, Clare Sibley 84
Burton, Andrew Joseph 32
Carelock, Janine Jude 19
Caseres, Alex 64
photographer John E. Bithorn
Cassano, Christopher 90
Coffin, Marissa 51
Coffin, Michelle 51
Condon, Jack 14
Cooey, Rachel Dee 86
Covey, Matthew 60
DaLudding, Andrew Phillip R. 22
Daniell, Frederick 66
David, Sarah Elizabeth 76
Deere, Taylor Hope 16
photographer James Welch
Dillon, Kirk Coleman 31
Donnelly, Kaitlin T. 19
Dorey, Andrew 7
Duva, Bryan 14 & 38
Eckert, Zachery Coleman 8
Fanning, Spencer Ryan 64
Finley, Alexandra 58

Givens, Eric 10
Goldenberg, Samuel Joseph 72
photographer Marvin Brown
Gordon, Lindsay Sarah 87
Greeley, Bryce 45
Greeley, Gavin 45
Greeley, Grant 45
Gibson, Kevin 44
Griffiths, Kai Joseph 66
Hall, Kristyne 16
Harring, Nicholas 23
Harrington, Rebecca 54
Hause, Morgan Andrew 73
Henry, Garrett 33
Henry, Jared 62
Hestir, Haven Elizabeth 65
Iaquinta, Joseph Savario 91
Johnson, Cassandra 79
photographer Richard Latimer
Johnson, Chanel 49
Johnson, Sidney 49
Jones, Lorin Boys 20
Kavett, Katherine E 57
Killingsworth Gore, Andrea 52
Klenk, Colin 67
Lanoux, Morgan 88
Lasater, Megan Marie 12
Lathrop, Happy 17
Lewis, Avery 46
photographer Patricia Switzer
Limone, Danella 92
Limone, Paul 92
MacDonald, Tarah 55
Martel, Solange 18
Martin, Adam Chase 62
Martin, Alex Ryan 37
photograph courtesy
of Caston Studios, Richmond, VA
Mathews, Nickie 57
McMillan, Elizabeth C. 83
photographer Janet Steiner Roberts
Minkoff, Ryan 18
Moline, Heather Mae 69
photographer Jo Ellen Moline
Moulico, Michael George 44
Mullen, John 22
Mullen, David 22
Mullen, Nathan 22
Muth, Eric 70
Nisbitt, Savanah 21
Nixon, Katie Marie 24

Nye, Lauren Christy 75
Pensabene, James 61
Popko, Luke 34
Raczycki, Ivan 94
Reed, Mark 24
Richardson, Abby 48
Richardson, Jenna 26
photographer Molly Richardson
Roberts, Savannah 65
photographer Pam Hill
Romney, Andrew 28
photographer Don Busath
Rosenberg, Jake 89
photographer Jeff Rosenberg
Rubell, Jonathan 20
Ryno, Ashley Lynne 85
photographer Bruce Gallagher
Sackett, Kyle Allen 35
Sather, Paul 65
Scott, Brian 58
Shaughnessy, Patrick 72
Simonson, Trevor 55 & 89
Simpson, Sarah 26 & 42
Stephens, Leah Danyelle 56
Stosick, Evan Scott 43
Szalay, Tom 93
photograph courtesy
of San Diego Union
Templeton, Lucas Tyler 63
Thill, Eric J. 47
Thilman, Jeremy 39
Tinucci, Jack 63
Todd, Jessica Lee 60
Tonnemacher, Clayton William 13
Trimble, Katie 50
Trollinger, Elizabeth 68
Trollinger, Mary 68
Van Hoy, Bristol 71
Van Nus, Warren Christopher 29
Vance, Simon 53
Volla, Chrissie back cover
Von Denes, Chris 56
photographer Lura Von Denes
Wade, Matthew back cover
Williams, Meishca 59
Worby, Mitchell James 11
Wray, Jeremy 74
Wray, Justin 74
Zaba, Audra 81